Tatsuki Fujimoto

I love *The Menu*!

Tatsuki Fujimoto won Honorable Mention in the
November 2013 Shueisha Crown Newcomers' Awards for
his debut one-shot story "Love Is Blind." His first series,
Fire Punch, ran for eight volumes. *Chainsaw Man* began
serialization in 2018 in *Weekly Shonen Jump*.

15

SHONEN JUMP Edition

Story & Art TATSUKI FUJIMOTO

Translation/AMANDA HALEY
Touch-Up Art & Lettering/SABRINA HEEP
Design/JULIAN [JR] ROBINSON
Editor/ALEXIS KIRSCH

CHAINSAW MAN © 2018 by Tatsuki Fujimoto
All rights reserved.
First published in Japan in 2018 by SHUEISHA Inc., Tokyo.
English translation rights arranged by SHUEISHA Inc.

The stories, characters, and incidents mentioned in this publication are
entirely fictional.

Printed in the U.S.A.

Published by VIZ Media, LLC
P.O. Box 77010
San Francisco, CA 94107

10 9 8 7 6 5 4 3 2 1
First printing, May 2024

PARENTAL ADVISORY
CHAINSAW MAN is rated T+ for Older Teen
and is recommended for ages 16 and up.
This volume contains violence and gore.

CHAINSAW MAN

15

Hors D'oeuvre

Tatsuki Fujimoto

CHARACTERS

Asa Mitaka

A lonely, bullied young woman who doesn't fit in at school. She was killed by the Justice Devil, but came back to life when the War Devil, Yoru, took over her body. Asa hates devils—they killed her parents—and she's no fan of Chainsaw Man either. Her current battle? Handling Yoru!!

Yoru (War Devil)

This War Devil's true form is owllike, but she hopped into Asa's body and claimed half of the human's brain. See, she's on a mission to kill Chainsaw Man...but if she wants to track him down, she'll need help blending into human society. She has the power to transform things she kills into weapons.

Denji (Chainsaw Man)

Chainsaw Man! He carries the Chainsaw Devil in his heart (literally). High schooler by day, vigilante devil hunter by night. Kishibe from Public Safety entrusted him with the new Control Devil, Nayuta...

Fami (The Famine Devil)

A mysterious member of the devil hunter club at Asa's school. She's the sister of the War Devil.

Hirofumi Yoshida

A devil hunter who belongs to a particular organization. Wants to keep Denji's identity under wraps.

STORY

Asa Mitaka is a lonely young woman who doesn't fit in at school. Even the class president, the closest person she has to a friend, hates Asa so much that she makes a contract with the Justice Devil and murders her. But that's when the War Devil, Yoru, takes over Asa's body, giving her a second chance at life! Yoru's on a mission to find Chainsaw Man, and she claims she'll return Asa's body if they can kill him...

In order to turn Denji into a weapon, Asa asks him out on a date at the aquarium. However, due to the Eternity Devil sent by Fami, Asa, Denji, Yoshida, and others become trapped there. While things start looking grim, Asa is able to turn the situation around with some quick thinking. Afterward, Asa tries to become closer with Denji, but her failure at human interaction causes her to despair.

Meanwhile, Fami tells Yoshida of the terrible fate that is about to befall the world. And at the same time, a terrifying primal devil makes its appearance...

CONTENTS

OH?

OH...

...DEAR.

WO

OO

I'M BEING QUITE INDECENT.

Chapter 123: Hors D'oeuvre

NOW THEN, ALLOW ME TO BEGIN COOKING.

ASA! SNAP OUT OF IT!

THAT DEVIL'S POWER IS CAUSING YOUR NEGATIVE FEELINGS!

...MY HORS D'OEUVRE, LA ROOT VONLA.

FOR THE FIRST COURSE, IT WILL BE MY PLEASURE TO FEED YOU...

OF THE TWO OF US, ONLY YOU CAN CREATE STRONG WEAPONS!

ARE YOU LISTEN- ING?!

CLAP

WHAT IS IT, MA'AM?

ASA, CAN WE TALK?

WHY DON'T WE HAVE MY FRIEND WHO LIKES CATS TAKE HIM?

IT'S ABOUT YOUR CAT.

ONE OF THE OTHER KIDS IS ALLERGIC.

HUH?

THIS IS UNHEALTHY FOR YOU TOO. YOU DEPEND ON THAT CAT'S COMPANIONSHIP INSTEAD OF INTERACTING WITH OTHER PEOPLE.

I DON'T WANNA.

DEVILS KILLED THEIR PARENTS.

ALL THE ORPHANS HERE...

MINE TOO.

MY MOM WAS KILLED BY THAT RECENT TYPHOON DEVIL.

WHERE'S
YOUR
CAT?

WHY?

WHAT?

ASA,
ARE YOU
ASLEEP?

...THERE
WAS A
CAT LIKE
YOURS...

CUZ
WHEN WE
WENT TO
THE RIVER
TO PLAY
TODAY...

...AT THE
BOTTOM.

ASA!
I CAN'T
ENTER
YOUR
BODY!!

DON'T
BE
AFRAID!!

Chapter 124: Soup

THUMP

ASA, YOU FOCUS ON THE PAIN IN YOUR FINGER.

IT'LL KEEP YOUR FEAR AT BAY.

I STILL FALL DOWN-WARD... THOUGHT SO.

NO, THIS DEVIL MAKES YOUR HAIR STAND ON END.

GRAVITY.

THE DEVIL'S NAME IS... TRAUMA.

A TRAUMATIC FLASHBACK, FOLLOWED BY...

THE FEAR IS MORE PRIMAL THAN THAT.

SUICIDE ---

MOON ---

SOME OF THE HUMANS ARE UNAFFECTED.

...RE-VERSED GRAVITY?

FALLING?

OR FAMINE'S INTERFERENCE AGAIN?

WHY DID SHE APPEAR HERE?

IS IT COINCIDENCE?

OWWW!!

ONLY THINK ABOUT THE PAIN. UNDERSTAND?

IT HURTS, NO?

THAT HURTS.

I'M DESPERATELY TRYING TO KEEP YOUR BODY ALIVE HERE!!

WHY FEAR ME *NOW*?!

YOU'RE AFRAID OF ME!!

YOU DROVE ME OUT OF YOUR BODY AGAIN!!

TRUST ME, YOU IDIOT !!

STUPID ?!

TRUST YOU?!

HOW CAN I, STUPID?!

YOU CUT MY HAND!!

I DON'T KNOW THE FIRST THING ABOUT YOU!

YOU'RE ALWAYS SAYING SCARY THINGS AND YOU TAKE OVER MY BODY WHENEVER YOU WANT AND—!

BECAUSE YOU'RE AFRAID!

YOU CUT MY HAND!!

WITH MY AGILITY, WE MIGHT ESCAPE.

YOUR FEAR JEOPARDIZES YOUR SURVIVAL.

THE DEVIL'S POWER IS MAKING YOU NEGATIVE.

THINK THIS THROUGH RATIONALLY.

YOU CAN LOOK INSIDE MY MIND AND SEE, RIGHT...?

WHAT I'M REALLY AFRAID OF.

I HAVE TRUST ISSUES, BUT I'M LONELY...

...SO ONCE IN A WHILE I'LL APPROACH SOMEONE...

...BUT SOMETHING *ALWAYS* GOES WRONG...

...AND I GET HURT...

...AND THEN I WIND UP ALL ALONE AGAIN!

MNGH!
MNGH!

FOR THE SOUP COURSE, I PRESENT DE ROOT ATELANTA.

A POTAGE MADE FROM THE EARS, TONGUE, AND NOSE OF A DEVIL HUNTER WHO TRIED TO HUNT ME.

Chainsaw
man

Chapter 125: Apple Thief

TEN EYES.

FOUR EARS.

THAT LEAVES ...

EXCUSE ME, DO YOU HAVE AN APPLE VARIETY THAT PAIRS WELL WITH HUMAN FLESH?

NOW, ABOUT THOSE APPLES ...

OH DEAR. PLEASE, RELAX.

UNLESS YOU ATTACK ME FIRST, I MEAN YOU NO HARM.

I'M SHORRY... I'M SHORRY...

THE RECIPE FOR THE SAUCE CALLED FOR A MAN'S HEAD.

GOODNESS, ME. I FORGOT.

EXCUSE ME, COULD SOMEBODY SPARE ME ONE?

CEASE
FIRE.

Chapter 126: Food Fight

...AND THEN I'LL TAKE MY LEAVE.

MY FINAL TASK IS TO DROP ASA MITAKA INTO HELL...

I WON'T KILL ANY MORE HUMANS. THERE'S NO NEED FOR US TO FIGHT.

YOU MUST BE CHAINSAW MAN.

DID YOU SAY...

...DROP ASA MITAKA INTO HELL?

THAT'S RIGHT.

GYAAA-
AAAH?!

BZZZ

ZZ

GRGH
...!

SPLRT

SPLRT

flik

YIPE!

I DETEST UGLI-NESS.

skwrt skwrt skwrt skwrt

GET... BACK ...

... HERE ...

fsh

...CHAINSAW MAN.

I STILL NEED YOU TO FIGHT...

ASA!

creak

GNNGH!

I CAN TELL BY THE WAY YOUR MUSCLES MOVE. BY THE SMELL OF YOUR SWEAT.

YOUR ATTACHMENT TO LIFE IS WEAK TO BEGIN WITH, NO?

WHAT TRULY SCARES YOU RIGHT NOW IS THE SHOCK OF THE IMPACT.

THE DARKNESS OF THE SKY. THAT'S ALL.

THE PHYSICAL SENSATION OF FALLING.

CLOSE YOUR EYES...

...AND I CAN PROMISE YOU A PEACEFUL FALL.

OH...

BUT I DO
HAVE ONE
REGRET.

EVEN ONE
PERSON...

EVEN IF IT
WAS WITH
ONLY ONE
PERSON,
WITH ALL
MY HEART,
I WISH I'D...

I WON'T
HAVE TO
CAUSE
TROUBLE
FOR
ANYONE
ELSE...

...OR
GET MY
FEELINGS
HURT
ANYMORE.

I WON'T
HAVE
TO LIE
IN BED...

...THINKING
ABOUT
ALL THE
THINGS I
DID WRONG
AS I WAIT
TO FALL
ASLEEP.

I'M OKAY WITH FALLING!! I ACCEPT IT!!

GETTING MADE INTO A FOOL, GETTING YOUR EXPEC-TATIONS UP ONLY TO BE LET DOWN!

LIFE IS NOTHING BUT PAIN!!

ISN'T IT?!

ARE YOU NUTS?!

WELL, YEAH, BUT, LIKE....!

WHOA—AH?!

Ice
cream!
Ice
cream!

We
stopped!
Cats!
Cats!

NNNNGH
....!

UHN!
UHHHN....!

DON'T MAKE ME REMEMBER CATS!

I KNOW HOW YOU FEEL!!

BELIEVE ME, I'VE BEEN THERE!!

NO ONE HAS IT WORSE THAN ME!!

WHAT WOULD YOU KNOW?!

JUST WHEN LIFE SEEMS SUPER AWESOME, AS SOON AS YOU LET YOUR GUARD DOWN...

...SOME CRAPPY THING HAPPENS OUTTA NOWHERE AND SCREWS IT ALL UP, RIGHT?!

YOU KNOW LIFE ISN'T **ALL** BAD...

...BUT DAY IN AND DAY OUT, ALL YOU CAN REMEMBER IS THE BAD STUFF...

...AND THE DISASTERS KEEP PILIN' UP LIKE A HAMBURGER MADE OF CRAP, RIGHT?

I'M NOT OVER IT!

I HAVEN'T!

--- CHAIN-SAW MAN?

HOW DID YOU GET OVER THAT...

WHAT'S THAT?

ONLY...

...I'VE GOT SOMETHING TO LIVE FOR! SOMETHING I LOOK FORWARD TO SO MUCH THAT I'M WILLING TO EAT THAT CRAPBURGER!

THINK ABOUT IT! HUMANITY GREW TO THIS SIZE CUZ SEX FEELS SO DAMN GOOD!

GROSS! YOU'RE A CREEP!

I CHANGED MY MIND! FORGET IT! GO TO HELL!!

WE'RE BOTH HERE NOW CUZ OF THE POWER OF SEX TOO!!

HUH?! IT'S NOT GROSS!!

Sex is, like, super beautiful!

LIKE, SOMEBODY ELSE'S SALIVA AND SWEAT ALL MIXING TOGETHER WITH YOURS?! IT'S JUST GROSS!!

PEOPLE ONLY HAVE SEX BECAUSE THEY HAVE NOTHING BETTER TO DO!!

Chapter 128: Main Dish

ARE YOU FOR REAL RIGHT NOW?!

WAIT... HUH?

WAIT A SEC. WHAT MAKES YOU EVEN THINK *YOU* WOULD EVER GET ANY?

NOTHING'S BETTER THAN SOMEBODY'S SALIVA AND SWEAT MIXING WITH YOURS!!

EVEN IF I CAN'T GET ANY RIGHT NOW...

HUH? ARE YOU FOR *REAL*?

...WHEN I'M OLDER, I'LL EVENTU-ALLY GET A GIRLFRIEND, AND THEN...

WHAP

MY MAIN DISH DOES NOT CALL FOR CHAINSAW MAN.

LEAVE ASA MITAKA AND I'LL SEND YOU BACK.

CAN I AT LEAST BRING HER ASS BACK WITH ME?

PERVERT.

THE FALLING DEVIL HAS NO TOLERANCE FOR DINERS WHO LEAVE THEIR FOOD UNFINISHED.

THEY'LL DESPERATELY TRY TO DEVOUR ASA MITAKA, LEST THEY BE KILLED BY THE FALLING DEVIL.

Chain saw man

Chapter 129: Save Me, Chainsaw Man

...CHAIN-SAW MANS?

TWO...

GAH!

FINISH HIM WHILE HE'S DOWN!!

ASA! NOW'S OUR CHANCE!

GHK!

YOU'LL FINALLY BE RID OF ME!!

KILL HIM AND I'LL RETURN YOUR BODY!!

JUST WHEN I'D FINALLY BEGUN TO UNDERSTAND YOU.

I SCREWED UP...

YOU ALWAYS DO THIS!

WHY...

...MUST YOU ALWAYS DO THE OPPOSITE OF WHAT I SAY?!

OWWW ?!

drip

YOU DON'T HAVE TO TAKE IT SO FAR AS TO SAVE MY MORTAL ENEMY!!

YOU'RE CROSS- ING THE LINE!!

...CHAIN- SAW MAN HAS SAVED MY LIFE TWICE NOW!

BETWEEN THAT TIME WITH YUKO AND TONIGHT...

BESIDES, WATCHING CHAINSAW MAN MAKES ME THINK...

...IF A PIECE OF TRASH LIKE HIM IS ALLOWED TO KEEP LIVING...

...THEN MAYBE IT'S OKAY FOR *ME* TO LIVE TOO!

THAT'S WHY—

ASA!!

HOW IS THE TASTE...

...OF HUMAN STEEPED IN FEAR?

I MADE
THAT
MEAL
WITH
LOVE...

I....
I MUH—

...
THROW
IT
UP?!

HOW
DARE
YOU...

I CONTROLLED THAT DEVIL'S BRAIN A TEENSY BIT...

...TO MAKE HUMANS TASTE LIKE LITERAL CRAP.

CONTROL.

WHY ARE YOU AFTER DENJI AND THIS GIRL...

...SIS?

NOSTRADA-MUS'S PROPHECY IS COMING TRUE.

THE ULTIMATE TERROR WILL SOON DESCEND ON THIS WORLD.

I LIKE THE SOUND OF THAT!

SOUNDS FUN!

IF THAT HAPPENS, THE AGE OF HUMANS WILL END...

I DON'T WANT IT.

...USHERING IN AN AGE OF DEVILS.

WHY NOT?

WHAT?! No way! No more pizza?!

...THINGS LIKE PIZZA AND CHINESE FOOD WILL CEASE TO BE.

IF AN AGE OF DEVILS COMES...

IT'S THE WORST SCENARIO IMAGINABLE.

I KNOW.

...NOR CHAINSAW MAN WILL BE ABLE TO STOP THE PROPHECY.

...NOR YOU...

AT THIS RATE, NEITHER I...

BUT...

...WAR DEVIL COULD...

...BE MADE TO WIN...

...POSSIBLY.

WORK WITH ME, CONTROL.

YOU JUST TRIED TO KILL HER!

WHAT GIVES?!

MY INTENTION WAS ONLY TO STARVE WAR IN THAT DEVIL'S BELLY.

WITH OUR STRENGTH COMBINED, THE AGE OF DEVILS MAY NOT ARRIVE.

I CAN TURN THE STARVED INTO MY PAWNS.

WHY NOT?

No way!

CUZ I HAVE SCHOOL!

Chapter 132: Protection

SHOTA, YUMI.

GIMME YOUR DES- SERTS.

HERE.

'KAY.

MIU DIED TOO...

IS IT JUST ME OR ARE A LOT OF KIDS ABSENT TODAY?

SHE'S MISSING, YOU MEAN!

LIKE, MORE KIDS ARE PROBABLY DEAD THAN ARE MOVING, DON'T YOU THINK?

I HEARD A LOT OF PEOPLE ARE MOVING AWAY FROM TOKYO.

DASH

OH REALLY ...

Power outages continue to affect all districts of the Tokyo Metropolitan area...

...with planned blackouts scheduled for the districts above.

Report any persons inciting fear during the confusion to this number...

At this time, confirmed casualties and missing persons exceed 2,000.

Gravity fluctuations caused by the Falling Devil's appearance are triggering cave-ins and landslides one after another across the world!

It isn't Japan alone!

Who is it that beat both the Falling Devil and the Gun Devil?! That's right— *Chainsaw Man!*

In a world veering toward apocalypse, can we really count on politicians and devil hunters?!

I AND THOSE WHO THINK LIKE ME FOUNDED AN ORGANIZATION! ITS NAME IS...

CHAINSAW MAN SAVES US FOR NO REWARD! AND I WANT TO WORK WITH HIM!

THE CHAINSAW MAN CHURCH FOR WORLD PEACE!

THE CHAINSAW MAN CHURCH IS NOW RECRUITING TALENT TO FIGHT ALONGSIDE CHAINSAW MAN!

HELP US PREVENT THE COMING PROPHECY OF NOSTRA- DAMUS!

FIGHT WITH US AT THE FORE- FRONT!

WHOOO!!

OH! PEACE!

CAREFUL, NOW! IF YOU FAIL COLLEGE ENTRANCE EXAMS BEFORE THE END OF THE WORLD...

...YOUR *LIFE* IS GONNA END FIRST!

HEY, YOU'RE STILL IN SCHOOL, RIGHT?

YOU REALLY BUY THIS NOSTRA-DAMUS STUFF?

ISEUMI, WAS IT?

Ан на на на на на на!!

На на на на на на!!

FAMI!

DID I REALLY HAVE TO APPEAR ON THAT LOWBROW VARIETY SHOW?!

DAMMIT!!

THEY SPUN MY EVERY WORD INTO MATERIAL FOR THE HOST'S JOKES!!

WHY?!

YOU DON'T NEED TO THINK.

RELAX.

THE RIDICULE WAS THE POINT.

YOUR JOB IS TO BE THE FACE.

FAMI IS THE BRAINS.

TOGETHER, YOU MOVE THE BODY— THE CHAINSAW MAN CHURCH.

IT'S LIKE FAMI SAYS.

...WALK TOWARD A WORLD WITHOUT EVIL, AREN'T YOU?

AND WITH THAT BODY, YOU'RE GONNA...

IT'S ALL FOR CHAINSAW MAN'S SAKE...

YES... I KNOW...

GOSH, THIS IS A RELIEF, DENJI.

YOU CALL THIS PROTECTION? FALLING ASLEEP IN CLASS ONLY TO WAKE UP TIED TO SOME CHAIR?

I'M GLAD I GOT YOU TO PROTECTION SAFE AND SOUND.

THEY SAID HER INJURIES ARE MINOR.

ASA MITAKA IS IN THE HOSPITAL.

WHAT ABOUT THE DOGS?

WHERE'S NAYUTA?

Chain saw man

Chapter 133: Chainsaw Man Protest

THEY'RE CALLING FOR PUBLIC SAFETY TO TREAT CHAINSAW MAN AS A DEVIL. TO PUT HIM DOWN.

I WANTED TO SHOW YOU THESE PROTESTERS.

OH!

BECAUSE THEY DON'T LIKE YOU.

BUT WHY? I'M A GOOD BOY.

THOSE GUYS CLASHING WITH THE PROTESTORS ARE FOLLOWERS OF THAT CHAINSAW MAN CHURCH THING, RIGHT?

BECAUSE THEY LIKE YOU.

WHY ARE THEY FIGHTING THE PROTESTORS?

...HAVIN' PEOPLE FIGHT OVER ME.

FEELS KINDA NICE...

RECENTLY, THOUGH, INCREASING NUMBERS OF YOUNG PEOPLE ARE JOINING JUST FOR THE HELL OF IT. I'M TOLD MEMBERSHIP NOW EXCEEDS 20,000.

BEFORE, THE CHAINSAW MAN CHURCH CONSISTED LARGELY OF YOUR FANS AND DEVIL VICTIMS.

APPARENTLY POLITICIANS ARE ALREADY STARTING TO CONTRIBUTE SUPPLIES TO THE CHURCH TOO.

THE BULK OF THEM ARE STILL IN SCHOOL, BUT EVENTUALLY, THEY'LL BE OLD ENOUGH TO VOTE.

HOPEFULLY IT WILL STOP AT THESE SMALLER PROTESTS, BUT THERE IS A CHANCE OF CHAINSAW MANIA EVOLVING INTO A LARGER CONFLICT.

YOU NO LONGER HAVE SOLE CONTROL OVER CHAINSAW MAN.

WHAT'S THAT MEAN?

I WANT YOU TO DO ABSOLUTELY NOTHING.

AND? WHAT DO I GOTTA DO TO SEE NAYUTA AND THE DOGS?

I'M ASKING YOU TO NEVER TRANSFORM INTO CHAINSAW MAN AGAIN.

HELL, NO.

I HEARD THAT YOU LONG TO LIVE A NORMAL LIFE.

SIMPLY STOP TRANS- FORMING, AND THAT DREAM COMES TRUE...

...WITH NAYUTA AT YOUR SIDE.

THIS IS YOUR CHANCE TO BE HUMAN AGAIN, DENJI.

is a devil!

I WANT EVERYBODY TO PAY ATTENTION TO ME!

BUT I...I *WANNA* BE CHAINSAW MAN!

DID YOU UNDERSTAND ME?

IF YOU TURN INTO CHAINSAW MAN, PUBLIC SAFETY WILL KILL NAYUTA.

DON'T YOU CARE IF NAYUTA DIES?!

PROTES-TORS, assemble!!

KILL THIS GUY FOR ME!!

DEN-JIII!!

HE'S EVEN DUMBER THAN I THOUGHT!

I...! I WANT PEOPLE TO FIGHT PROTESTORS FOR ME!!

I DON'T WANT THAT EITHER!

LOOK, DENJI...

THE TIME HAS COME FOR YOU TO CHOOSE...

...BETWEEN NAYUTA'S LIFE...

...AND YOUR GREEDY DESIRES.

BUT I ALSO DON'T WANNA STOP BEING CHAINSAW MAN!!

HUH? YOU WEREN'T DONE YET?

IT'S TOO SOON TO LET THEM MEET!!

YOU STINK!

CUZ I HAVEN'T HAD A BATH!

WHY ---?!

LISTEN TO ME, DENJI!!

YOU WERE ABOUT TO CHOOSE NAYUTA'S LIFE AND GET SENT HOME TOGETHER!

EX-CUSE ME?!

WHATEVER! THIS MUST HAVE PROVEN IT TO YOU!

Denji! Tell this guy to eff off!!

Now!!

IF YOU TURN INTO CHAINSAW MAN, PUBLIC SAFETY *WILL* KILL NAYUTA!!

YOU DONE?! THEN WE'RE GOIN' HOME!

DID HE NOT UNDER-STAND ME?

TO BE CONTINUED...

CHAINSAW
MAN

Variety Show

OH... THAT GIRL WHO JUST APPEARED ON THE SHOW IS REALLY CUTE...

WELL... IF I LEARNED SOME MAKEUP TRICKS AND WORKED ON MY HAIR, I COULD PROBABLY SURPASS HER.

BUT THAT'S A LOT OF WORK, AND IT'S NOT LIKE I WANT TO BE CUTE. SO, IT'S NOT BECAUSE I CAN'T, I JUST DON'T WANT TO.

THAT GIRL'S ONLY ATTRIBUTE IS BEING CUTE, BUT I'M ALSO PRETTY SMART. SO OVERALL, I'M AHEAD OF HER.

Movie

THIS ACTRESS IS REALLY GOOD...

WAIT... BUT BEING A GOOD ACTRESS MEANS YOU'RE A GOOD LIAR. SO THAT'S NOT REALLY A GOOD THING FOR YOUR EVERYDAY LIFE...

IF I PRACTICED REALLY HARD, I COULD PROBABLY BECOME AN ACTRESS, BUT I DON'T WANT TO BECAUSE I AM AGAINST LYING... THOUGH IF SOMEONE OFFERED ME A JOB, I MIGHT DO IT...

DO YOU EVER SHUT UP?

THE CELEBRITY LIFESTYLE CAN REALLY MESS YOU UP, SO I PROBABLY HAVE AN OVERALL BETTER LIFE THAN HER. SO, I'M GLAD I'VE NEVER BEEN APPROACHED ON THE STREET BY SCOUTS. THOUGH IF I DID BECOME AN ACTRESS, OVERALL, I WOULD BE....

YOU'RE READING THE WRONG WAY!

Chainsaw Man reads from right to left, starting in the upper-right corner. Japanese is read from right to left, meaning that action, sound effects, and word-balloon order are completely reversed from English order.